Ernst Pauer

The Elements of the Beautiful in Music

Ernst Pauer

The Elements of the Beautiful in Music

ISBN/EAN: 9783337089146

Printed in Europe, USA, Canada, Australia, Japan

Cover: Foto ©Thomas Meinert / pixelio.de

More available books at **www.hansebooks.com**

Imperial Octavo, 460 pp. Handsomely bound in Cloth, gilt edges, price 16s.

A DICTIONARY

OF

MUSICAL TERMS

EDITED BY

J. STAINER, M.A., Mus. D/p0.,

MAGD. COLL., OXFORD,

AND

W. A. BARRETT, Mus. Bac

S. MARY HALL, OXFORD.

The following Ge. : contributed to this Work.

BOSANQUET, R. H. ' :
M.A., Fellow of St. J.
Oxford.

ULLEY, J., Es.
dalen College, O

CHAMPNEYS,
M.A., M.R.C.S.,
mew's Hospital
Travelling Fellow
versity of Oxford.

CHAPPELL, W., Es.

DONKIN, A. E., Esq., M.A.,
F.R.A.S., Fellow of Exeter
College, Oxford.

LIS, A. J., Esq., B.A., F.R.S.,
G.A., F.C.P.S., F.C.P., Trinity
College, Cambridge.

DSBY, HENRY, Esq.

MORE, Rev. T., M.A.

LAH, JOHN, Esq.

AUGHT, W. G., Esq.

K, W. H., Esq.

LONDON: NOVELLO, EWER & CO.

EDITOR'S PREFACE.

IN issuing this series of Music Primers the Editor sees with pleasure the realisation of a desire he has long felt, to place in the hands of teachers and students of music a set of educational works of a high standard at a price so low as to render them attainable by all.

The growing interest in music generally, and rapid spread of its study, so very evident in this country, render it of the utmost importance that the student's first steps in every branch should be directed with skill and based on sound principles. The Editor has kept this object steadily in view, and he believes that each one of these Primers will prove to be as carefully constructed in detail as it is comprehensive in design.

Such a result would have been impossible but for the hearty support and sympathy of those authors, men of known ability in their special branches of art, who have embodied the results of their long and valuable experience in their respective contributions.

While gratefully acknowledging the kindness of these gentlemen, the Editor cannot but express a hope that the Primers may prove as useful to the public, and as beneficial to art, as both authors and publishers have endeavoured to make them.

SECOND EDITION.

NOVELLO, EWER AND CO.'S MUSIC PRIMERS
EDITED BY DR. STAINER.

THE ELEMENTS

OF THE

EAUTIFUL IN MUSIC

BY

ERNST PAUER

*Principal Professor of the Pianoforte at the National Training School for
Music, South Kensington.*

PRICE ONE SHILLING.

LONDON: NOVELLO, EWER AND CO.,
I, BERNERS STREET (W.), AND 80 AND 81, QUEEN STREET (E.C.)

BOSTON, NEW YORK, AND PHILADELPHIA:
DITSON AND CO.

NOVELLO, EWER AND CO.,
TYPOGRAPHICAL MUSIC AND GENERAL PRINTERS,
I, BERNERS STREET, LONDON.

PREFACE.

To one who has devoted his life to the study of music, it may often be a subject of curious consideration, whether the unconscious admiration of a fine work—the unreasoning enthusiasm for a certain composer—the complacent feeling of enjoyment produced in the majority of those who listen to masterpieces in music—may not indeed be a state of mind which it would be cruel to disturb. But then comes the consideration, how much greater must be the enjoyment and pleasure derived from a "thing of beauty" if we are able to analyse the elements of this beauty and to justify our own admiration! How much our respect for the composer will increase if, instead of "wondering with a foolish face of praise," we can understand the relations between the author and the musical art, and render to ourselves an account of our enthusiasm, by investigating and appreciating the laws and rules that govern the Beautiful! This consideration must impress us with the necessity and usefulness of an analysis of the Beautiful in Music.

Many volumes have at various times been written on the nature of Beauty. Plato, Aristotle, Pythagoras, Longinus, Dante, Kant, Hegel, Schelling, Oersted, and many others have examined the question; and of late, also, much has been written to throw light on a subject which, although its rules are fixed and definite, allows a great latitude of personal or relative

opinion. The immediate purpose of this little work is to eluci-
date and illustrate the laws and rules which must be observed in
constructing a really perfect and beautiful musical work of art.

The subject must be divided into three distinct parts, each
of which occupies a large field, and requires an attentive and
careful examination and discussion. It is exhaustively treated
in the valuable work, " Æsthetics of Music," by Professor Hand.
The learned professor evolved his theory chiefly from philosophical
principles.

This short treatise is based upon Hand's work ; but I have
found it necessary, for practical purposes, to treat the subject from
a more popular point of view, with regard especially to musical
practice.

E. PAUER.

39c, ONSLOW SQUARE, LONDON, S.W., 1877.

CONTENTS.

INTRODUCTORY REMARKS.

In everything that concerns musical art, we have to recognise three especial points: *a free form, a full and vigorous life*, and *an ideal animation.* We may call these the three *constituent elements* of the art. But we have not to consider these parts as three different principles, but as comprising and containing one principle only. This principle is also to be regarded from three different points of view, according to the three elements, which, taken together, constitute a perfect work of art. Every production of art must first of all be considered as a *thing*, and consequently as having a *form;* secondly, it is to be considered as a *separate thing*, and consequently as possessing its own *separate* and *individual character;* and, thirdly, it must be considered in reference to a *general motive* or *design*, in so far as it *originates* or *reproduces* an *idea*, which it has partly or wholly incorporated. A beautiful work of art must necessarily possess perfection of appearance or form, reality, and an ideal life. We therefore recognise a threefold beauty—that of *form*, of *character*, and of *idea.* The essence of formal beauty is *harmony;* that of characteristic beauty, *expression;* and that of ideal beauty, *power of imagination*, which latter accordingly is designated by the term *ideality.* The possession of this ideality, united to a love of the beautiful, is, in its higher development, one of the chief constituents of creative genius. A real and perfect work of art results from the union of these three elements or qualities, and not one of them can be dispensed with ; but according as one or another may preponderate, or appear in greater prominence, we judge of the peculiar or specific quality of any separate work. Where these elements are found in the highest perfection, they reciprocally influence each other in equal proportions ; and then only do those three chief elements of the Beautiful—the *formal*, the *characteristic*, and the *ideal*—appear thoroughly in accordance. We have now to examine the nature of these three musical qualities or elements; and we proceed in the first place to consider the subject of Formal Beauty

THE BEAUTIFUL IN MUSIC.

I.

FORMAL BEAUTY.

WE designate as "formal" that beauty in which we recognise the perfection of construction. The word formal is here employed in the sense of "belonging to form," and not as synonymous with "conventional" or "constrained." This free form must be built upon a systematic and well-laid foundation; there must be a perfect unity, harmony, and proportion of all the component parts; and thus the work will be endued with a harmonious life. Mere mechanical dexterity, without intellectual activity and genius, will result in a regularity, confined to the outward appearance of the work, and perhaps mathematically faultless and correct, but yet destitute of beauty. We may take for instance the most correctly constructed exercises in harmony or thorough-bass—they will certainly not impress the hearer with the feeling of beauty; just as a regular combination of mathematical lines would not necessarily constitute a pleasing drawing or a graceful design. Any one who desires to see a good example of regularity, correctness, and excellent workmanship, may find it in the fugues of Albrechtsberger, at one time the teacher of Beethoven; but for beauty let these mechanical productions be compared, or rather contrasted, with the fugues of Sebastian Bach. The impression of formal beauty emanates from an inward consciousness and appreciation of order, symmetry, and proportion in a work. This feeling of order must be an instinct with the composer, and must be felt by the hearer; unconsciously indeed, but in such a complete degree that the sense is thoroughly satisfied, and the hearer feels no desire to examine or to measure the work in the way of testing the rules, or analysing the method of construction. So soon as there arises in the hearer the desire to investigate the correctness and the systematic observance of the rules, the composition may be called regular, but certainly cannot be called positively and undeniably beautiful; it lacks the spirit of freedom, of independence, inseparable from beauty.

Were we, for instance, to divide the surface of a statue into squares, its beauty would certainly vanish; and very similar would be the result were we to reduce a sonata of Beethoven into mere numbers: we should simply miss its beauty. It is not the aim of music to become a demonstration of mathematical power; it ought to be and to remain _poetry in sounds._ This maxim we especially recognise in fugues, a form which originally depends on abstract rules; and yet such men as Sebastian Bach understood how to infuse into these apparently mechanical works a spirit of freedom and beauty, so that we admire the performance, and are actually not aware that we are listening to a work eminently representative of the scientific or mathematical part of music. Bach in his fugues compels the sounds to obey his will; whilst in other fugues the sounds, so to speak, bear away the composer as a helpless prisoner, compelled to follow them.

A piece of music may be constructed with such absolute beauty of form that the sense of order and symmetry will be pleased, though the heart of the hearer is not warmed or elevated by it; just as an essay may be written with such exquisite elegance, clearness, and polish of style that we admire it for these merits, and yet do not feel a higher interest in the contents of the work. An example is seen in Hummel's celebrated Duet-Sonata in A flat. It is a model of perfection as regards smoothness and harmony of form, and yet it leaves us cold and unimpressed.

Correctness can only be raised to beauty by the addition of variety, of diversity, and by appearing in different phases and degrees; a composition that is devoid of this diversity of thought will remain, as Pope designated many of the productions of his contemporaries, "correctly dull and regularly low." Thus a duet, which moves only in thirds or sixths, might possess the merit of being set according to rule, but certainly would not rouse our interest, or be agreeable to our æsthetic feeling. The desire in the hearer to measure, to examine the form, must be charmed away by the genius of the composer. The hearer must intuitively feel the presence of rule and order, without desiring to analyse them; and yet, were we to analyse or dissect a sonata of Mozart or Beethoven, we should be astonished to find how all the free movement that delights us is kept within the rigorous bounds of strict and well-defined rule. Here the intellect does not feel the necessity of analysis; the hearer's sympathy is aroused and maintained by the excellence of the composition. Who would measure the lines of Shakespeare with a foot-rule to see if each contained the correct number of long and short syllables? This magnetic attraction, this power of enchaining attention, is a mysterious gift, and can only be described as the irresistible sway exercised by _genius._ A discordant element becomes perceptible when a single part fails to harmonise with the others; then the hearer's feeling of symmetry is disturbed. A spasmodic use of discords, for instance, badly prepared and unnecessarily repeated, will produce a disagreeable impression; whilst a proper and rational use of discords, and their alternation with concords, will gratify the ear, as the natural expression of a pleasing, and indeed an indispensable contrast. It is the antithesis of the discord and concord which fascinates and charms the ear; it is the necessary solution and the return to unity which delights us. In this juxtaposition of opposites the true and accurate feeling of the composer finds its chief exponent; and here the true musician detects and seizes a ready opportunity to display the natural refinement of his art.

A perfect musical work could not exist without the use of discords; for these appear not only as a welcome relief, but as an actual necessity, to bring out the concord in full power, and rightly to display its importance. The experienced artist can thus with truth say that the discordant material under his hand becomes the chief ingredient of the beautiful.

Formal beauty does not strive to _free itself_ from the just responsibilities and the salutary limitation of order and rule, but merely tries to eliminate the tyrannical element that confines and oppresses. Where fancy does not recognise any limit or any order, it loses itself in cloudy indistinctness, and appears at last unhealthy or even absurd; on the other hand, where the rule is obtrusively predominant, the impression will be that of pedantry and stiffness. Thus Beethoven, Haydn, and Mozart were so intimately acquainted with the laws of the beautiful, and at the same time so convinced of the indispensableness of order and rule, that their fancy was always under the dominion of these laws, even in their boldest flights of originality.

In music, formal beauty can only appear in movement, in

progression; a *single tone* may be agreeable in itself, but taken alone is not beautiful: a *single chord* may be euphonious, but does not constitute music: only when tones and chords are blended together in union, the whole will gain life, and a musical entity will be formed. Even a *single melody* is not, strictly speaking, expressive of formal beauty; but it becomes an important element of the beautiful, and receives a more distinct importance, when it is combined with harmonies and incorporated in the whole. If a melody is to connect itself harmoniously with the structure of the whole piece, it is important to consider relation and contrast of key. The less harmonisation a melody requires to appear beautiful, the stronger will be its natural and independent charm. When a melody requires many changes of harmony to appear interesting and fascinating, it is in itself feeble and unsatisfactory. Still, no rule is without an exception. There are some melodies, so complete and perfect in themselves, that they are sufficient to satisfy the craving for the beautiful, without external ornament, and appear as instances of the axiom, "Beauty unadorned, adorned the most."

The harmonious changes and modulations in general, and the ideas as to the conditions under which they may be considered beautiful, have undergone important variations. Modulations which appeared to our forefathers as harsh, unnatural, and illogical, are readily accepted in our time, and are received without the least hesitation. No strict rule as to the *correctness* or *incorrectness* of certain modulations can be laid down; the natural and instinctive feeling of the refined hearer is always the best criterion; and Rossini's remark, "that what pleased his ears he considered good and correct," is in his case very apt and just. Real taste and true genius will never accept anything that is against the law of nature. It may be considered as an advantage that diversity of opinion and feeling exists in matters of taste. This diversity does not preclude the existence of necessary and rigid rules, to which even the most tolerant ear will pay unconscious homage.

In modulations there ought to be at least one tone, which acts, so to say, as the thread uniting it with the next. Another requirement for clearness and beauty is a well-balanced and natural relation of the melody to the bass; for the bass is the root of the harmony which forms its foundation and support;

therefore the composer will always treat it with due respect; but he will, on the other hand, be careful not to crush or drown the melody, or to retard its movement and interfere with its vitality by too great a prominence or monotony of the bass.

The melodious movement forms groups which are called figures; and in these figures various new melodies arise in a completely free and natural manner. The good taste and sound feeling of a composer is shown in the fact, that he will always keep in view the important principal theme or subject. A good composer uses the so-called tributary or companion melodies in a certain definite order. He arranges them in proportion to their respective interest, value, and beauty. No composer illustrates this maxim by such excellent and wonderful examples and models as we find in Beethoven; to mention only two among a great number, I would indicate his Quartett in F major (Op. 59), and his great Trio in B flat (Op. 97).

Too great a prominence of subordinate figures will destroy the beauty of the composition, and interfere with the adjustment of the necessary balance. The too great prevalence and repetition of figures in our modern compositions is a serious blot in modern music. The figure, used with taste and discrimination, is one of the readiest means of introducing beauty and charm into music; and no pleasure can be greater or more genuine than the delight of observing the gradual growth and development of figures out of the principal theme, and the appreciation of the important part they play in succession—how they enrich, vary, and consolidate the principal subject. This development resembles the organic growth and enlargement of a plant that unfolds its leaves and blossoms into beauty.

We find that figures—even more than harmony and melody— are subject to the influence of time, and to the variations of taste. If we examine an old piece of music, and are inclined to pronounce it obsolete or antiquated, we shall generally perceive that the antiquated nature shows itself more in the figures (which the French called most aptly *broderies*) than in the harmonies or in the melody. Many a piece of Handel, Corelli, or Scarlatti, sounds old-fashioned, whilst it possesses a vigorous and not antiquated substance, which, however, is surrounded with figures that grate harshly upon our present taste. In fact, the figure is the garb in which the composer clothes his thought.

It is exceedingly difficult to define precisely and appropriately the meaning and the office of a leading musical idea. The art of music belongs to the realm of feeling; the leading idea may be called a tone-picture which portrays a certain emotion, and which, as every part of it admits of different associations, is capable of very varied development. We call an idea poor when it consists of tones put together at random or by mere chance, and therefore wanting in that intellectual life which alone is able to excite our interest and sympathy.

As the principal idea is the starting-point of the entire composition, like the text given out for a sermon, the composer has to be careful to observe in it all the requirements of the beautiful. If the composer relies only on the laws of harmony, the consequence will be mere grammatical correctness, and nothing more; it is necessary that not only the composition be correct, but that beauty should pervade it. The principal idea, and the piece which results from it, must show a free form and an independent life, within harmoniously constructed and well-ordered conditions. All that has to be seized by our intellectual faculties, everything regular and systematic, should have free scope in the work: a certain life must be breathed into the whole. What was rigid ought to flow, what was cold and lifeless to breathe; intellectual life ought to be everywhere noticeable. In some of the modern pieces, instead of healthy and substantial ideas, there appears a vacuum, which affords an opportunity for the introduction of those elaborate passages in a barren work, which Beethoven used sarcastically to term " gymnastic evolutions." It is in the change of tones, in their height and depth, in their increasing and decreasing force, in the melodious connection of the respective periods and phrases, in figures and in harmonies, in the rhythmical movement, that the composer shows his aptitude to treat the chief idea in an artistic form, and to present the whole as a picture in which measure and freedom appear simultaneously; so that the pleased auditor recognises with delight the unity of different elements. Even in their indispensable contrast the component parts ought to incline towards each other; they may appear to be in contradiction, but each has its appropriate place in the organisation of the whole, and nothing is left to mere chance.

It is exceedingly interesting to observe how in musical

composition we meet with forms identical with those the literary writer introduces into his work, and which are commonly known as "figures and devices." In music *synonyms* may be said to occur in the varied expression of tones, whose signification is identical;—*epithet* there appears as a more detailed expression, or an elaboration of a figure;—*inversion*—in the variation in sequence to previously expressed form;—the "*asyndeton*" appears as the unconnected sequence;—the "*hyperbaton*" in the succession of various parts in apparent disorder, in repetitions of groups and phrases, in gradations towards a higher phase or tone, in inclination towards the profound;—the "*aposiopesis*" in the suddenly interrupted sequence;—the "*parenthesis*" in the interpolation of a new phrase into a passage already complete in itself. All these means of expression belong to the formal beauty, although some critics considered them as part of the characteristic expression. Thus, great composers have been blamed for what are called faults, but are in reality rather merits; at least, they are certainly not errors. Beethoven, for instance, has been censured for passing, in the scherzo of the Pastoral Symphony, from the key of F major into that of D major, without any preparation; he has likewise been found fault with for the stationary bass of the scherzo, and for the change of three-four time into that of two-four, which change occurs in the beginning of the trio. But these remarkable features are certainly not faults. Beethoven has here merely put the characteristic expression into the foreground; and, without disturbing the balance or the symmetry of his formal structure, he infuses into his piece a jovial and rustic expression; indeed, he penetrates it with a thoroughly pastoral character and tone. Another example is found in a composer who excelled in the power of wonderfully combining the formal with the characteristic beauty—namely, Sebastian Bach. In his dance-tunes, which we find scattered through his so-called French and English suites and partitas, the allemandes, courantes, sarabandes, gavottes, bourrées, and gigues, we are struck with the highly finished, thoroughly rounded, and polished form; whilst at the same time they also express in the happiest manner the characteristic features of their respective nationalities. The simplicity and the perfect unvarnished truthfulness in which these little masterpieces of Bach speak to us, have sometimes been mistaken for meagreness and poverty, whilst they are in reality the highest proof of a correct and accurate feeling. In listening to our great master's works, we are often surprised at the agreeable feeling of comfort and ease, of equanimity and calmness, which mingles with the entertainment and pleasure they afford; this agreeable feeling of contentment and genuine satisfaction is in no small degree owing to the innate order, the plastic roundness, which exists in these works. The ear feels unconsciously the exactitude and regularity with which the different parts, phrases, and sentences follow each other; just as the eye is pleased with the symmetrical dimensions, the exact proportions of a building, though it may be difficult definitely to analyse the pleasure this harmony of proportion affords.

Equally with the sequence of tones, the rhythmical form is subject to the rules of formal beauty; but in so far as rhythm, in which the tones appear and obtain significance, is bound to a systematic law or necessity, which we call measure or time, symmetry, to produce a good and beautiful effect, must evince itself in a free unrestricted movement; and the even proportions must enter into manifold combinations in such a way, that in the form given by rhythm, strict and limited though it be, we recognise an intellectual life. We may take, for instance, the scherzo of Beethoven's Eroica Symphony; its movement is exceedingly quick, and the rhythmical design the simplest possible— three crotchets in a bar. At first the attention is arrested by the rhythmical beat, and we listen with pleasure to that neat, accurate, and industrious pulse, which seems redolent with young life. But if Beethoven continued this quick repeated beat for any length of time, we should soon be tired by the monotony, and our interest would flag. But he makes it by degrees appear that this limited rhythm enlarges itself to greater dimensions; four bars are combined into one effect, and thus the ear is relieved from the narrow form, and we enter a wider field. After a time we have again forgotten this last rhythmical design, and are fascinated by the gradations of the harmonies, by the clever alternation of the effects produced by the different groups of wind and stringed instruments, which take up the theme alternately; indeed, a variety of interesting features work upon our intellectual faculties, which are delighted, refreshed, and fascinated by the constant change which appears here in music, like the prismatic sparkle in a diamond.   Such treatment is the best proof of a free and independent movement.   A mere repetition of the same figure must needs lead to monotony, and fatigue the hearer.

The consideration of the beauty that may be imparted by the performer to a musical work forms a very important part of the subject.   Every violation of the laws of rhythm naturally exercises an injurious effect upon melody and harmony, and may even, if such violation appears in prominent degree, result in the destruction of a musical work of art.   But on the other hand, the performance ought not to lack a legitimate freedom and independence, within the bounds of rule, as shown in the measure or bar.   *Freedom* of time must not be confounded with *licence*, or with *disregard* of time ; for freedom is the highest perfection or the ideal of legality and order, while licence leads to disorder and anarchy.   The alteration or dislocation of time at random, merely to suit and please the whim of an individual—or intended, in clap-trap fashion, to obtain by such extravagances the credit of an original reading—is inartistic and inadmissible, and shows a lamentable want of proper respect for the work to be interpreted.

As the syncopation, which means an inversion of the order of notes, or a prolonging of a note begun on the unaccented part of one bar, to the next bar, belongs to the domain of rhythm, it follows that it is also one of the component parts of formal beauty. The real and proper application of the syncopation is to be found in the domain of the characteristic.

In conclusion, it must be borne in mind that the chief ingredient of formal beauty is harmony.   This word harmony comprises in its entirety all that we have to recognise and to remember concerning formal beauty.   Lord Bacon says : "Equality and correspondence are the causes of harmony;"—and if we take up any sonata of Mozart or Beethoven, or any quartett or symphony of our great composers, we shall find that *equality* reigns in all the component parts, and that each phrase, sentence, modulation, &c., corresponds exactly, and in the most natural and complete manner with its predecessors; and thus harmony results.   Goethe says truly : " Every form, even the most pleasing, has something untrue in itself; but form is, after all, the glass in which we collect the sacred rays of diffused nature, and bring them together to kindle a fire in the hearts of mankind."

B

Perfection of form is the result of perseverance and of the earnest study of masters, whose characteristics every successor should try to understand as soon as possible. It would be an incorrect idea of originality, if every one were expected to grope about in his own way after new forms, to re-discover perhaps in an imperfect way what we possess already in the greatest perfection. By study the form is transmitted and imitated, and will perhaps be improved and purified ; and thus we recognise progress in art. Mozart improved the form used by Haydn ; Beethoven enlarged upon the form used by Mozart. If this were not the case, every one would have to begin anew ; but " art is long and time is fleeting," and therefore it is advisable to husband our powers, and to avail ourselves of what our predecessors have done for us. To seek progress only in new forms, is a doubtful practice. Goethe, in his practical and clear manner, says truly : " Genius conceives and understands the importance of form at once ; and it submits to its rules willingly and ungrudgingly. Only the smatterer, only the pretender, misled by vanity, will desire to substitute his limited peculiarity for the unconditional whole, and to excuse his wrong maxims under the plea of an irresistible feeling of originality and independence."

In music, where the sounds pass rapidly before our ear, a vigorous, decided, and concise form is an indispensable necessity, if the hearer is to receive and retain a definite impression of the whole and an insight into the working of a composition ; so that he may even recognise the smallest traits and what appear at first the most insignificant parts of a composition. No better advice can be given to the student than that he should take one of our great masterpieces, and carefully and conscientiously analyse it, reducing the composition to a skeleton, divesting it of all its elaboration and ornament, and striving to understand what are the most necessary and indispensable conditions of its existence. The student will thus become convinced that *order* and *symmetry* are the chief requisites of a production, whose aim is to afford a lasting satisfaction to the intelligent hearer. Such study, such careful and conscientious examination and investigation, will richly repay the trouble which it costs ; and the result will be not only satisfactory to the student's sense of order but will afford him an insight into the depths and secret ways of the musical art which he could in no other way have obtained.

II.

CHARACTERISTIC BEAUTY.

In Formal Beauty we recognise the first principle of the musical art; but taken alone it does not appear sufficient to fulfil all the conditions of a perfect work. The characteristic element is absolutely necessary, to infuse into the formal beauty that interest which alone gives it life and animation. The characteristic feature may be defined as that which marks or expresses the distinctive qualities of a person or of a thing. The law of characteristic beauty is expression and feeling, and these are the qualities that impart interest and importance to a work. Characteristic expression is therefore a highly important feature in the beautiful, and can on no account be dispensed with; for in a work it is the life and soul. Defects in the rules of formal beauty are of less importance than the want of characteristic expression. No composer illustrates this assertion better and more clearly in his works than the general favourite C. M. von Weber,—who, by no means perfect in regard to formal beauty, is still endowed with a great and undeniable fascination, and that simply through the fervour and animation of his characteristic expression.

In music, the innermost feelings of the composer are displayed; and in so far as the characteristic is founded on the individual or personal feeling, an original composition must in itself be characteristic. The characteristic shows itself by means of the tones and intervals, and finds expression through the minor and major keys, through the time and movement, through the accent, the rest, the figures, and passages, and last, but not least, through the melody. The high notes generally express the more lively and the brighter emotions of the soul; yet these higher notes may also portray anxiety, and even despair; whilst the lower notes express solemnity, calmness, dignity, and earnestness, a certain resignation, and an intense though chastened grief. There is also a physical reason for the more sedate and quiet expression in the deeper notes: namely, the slower vibration of the strings, which necessitates a slower progress of the harmonies or figures. If brilliant passages, intended for the

violin, were played on a tenor, we should be astonished at the
complete change of character produced, and at the loss of
brightness and distinctness that would ensue ; and the same
impression would be made, if songs intended by the composer for
a soprano voice were sung by a contralto. If we turn to the
intervals, we shall find that the fifth may be regarded as the
centre, although it does not possess any characteristic expression
except when associated with the third. The third is certainly
the most important interval with respect to characteristic
expression ;—it decides the expression, and renders it either
cheerful or melancholy. The major third expresses power,
quietness, and grandeur, concord and contentment ; the minor
third, on the other hand, gives an idea of tenderness, grief, and
romantic feeling. Although both thirds, major and minor, are
full of expression, a frequent repetition of them, or parallel
sequences, will result in monotony. If the third is given an
octave higher, or as a tenth, its expression is that of calmness
and dignity. The fourth expresses doubt and uncertainty, the
seventh a longing for a solution; the second lacks a definite
expression, whilst the diminished second sounds harsh ; the
expression of the sixth, major and minor, is almost identical
with that of the third. The expression of a single chord is
certainly not a grand one ; although we may recognise in the
major triad perfection and clearness, determination and solidity.
The diminished triad—

expresses indecision and doubt, and, like the interval of the
seventh, seems to demand a solution. The triad, in its first
position, appearing, namely, as a chord of the sixth, shows
greater brightness and grandeur ; whilst the chord ending with
the seventh is full of boldness and vigour, and requires a
solution, like the seventh as a single interval.

It would lead us too far, in a work like the present, to attempt
to point out the characteristic expression of every chord ; but it
is certainly necessary to remark on the different character or
expression apparent in the various keys.

The key is in music what colour is in painting. The key furnishes the tone to the piece ; and if we desire to be impartial
and conscientious judges, we ought always, particularly in the

case of songs, which for the convenience of singers are so often transposed, to inquire what was the original key in which the composer wrote his work. To give only one short example,— Mendelssohn's celebrated song "Auf Flügeln des Gesanges" ("On Song's bright pinions"), originally written in the key of A flat for a mezzo-soprano, loses its characteristic expression by being sung in F major, as adapted for a contralto. The different character of the various keys was already recognised by Plato and Aristotle, who both speak of keys which act in an enervating way, and of others which exert an awakening and invigorating influence on the human mind. We may take it for granted that every key has, to a certain extent, its particular domain, in which it reigns with a decided supremacy, and in which it satisfactorily expresses its individual character.

The proper choice of the key is of the utmost importance for the success of a musical work ; and we find that our great composers acted in this matter with consummate prudence and with careful circumspection. It would not be hypercritical, were we to recognise in the greater frequence of the use of a certain key a predilection or idiosyncrasy of the composer. Thus we find that Beethoven was undoubtedly partial to the key of C ; for when we look in the catalogue of his works and count his sonatas, duet-sonatas, quartetts, quintetts, overtures, symphonies, we find that he wrote twenty-five works in the key of C, fifteen in that of E flat, thirteen in that of F, thirteen in that of G, eleven in the key of D and A flat, nine in A, eight in B flat, five in E, three in C sharp, and only a solitary one in F sharp. In examining the thematic catalogue of Mozart's works, we find that most of his compositions are written in the keys of C, G, F, D, and B flat. Again, an examination of the keys used for slow movements will show us that Beethoven, more particularly in his first compositions, had a predilection for the key of A flat, and Mozart for that of F major.

Major keys express chiefly joy, power, brightness of feeling ; but they are also able to portray, in a highly effective manner, a quiet and melancholy expression ; and lend themselves readily to depict seriousness, dignity, and grandeur. Examples : the aria "Dove sono" in "Le Nozze di Figaro," Donna Anna's great scena and aria in F major in "Don Giovanni," and the great air of Agatna, "Softly sighs," in "Der Freischütz."

The expression of the minor keys is of an indefinite and suggestive character. Minor keys are chosen for expressing intense seriousness, soft melancholy, longing, sadness, and passionate grief; their colour may be called sombre, and when compared with that of the major keys, appears somewhat pale. The minor keys appeal directly to the feelings, but after some time, have a somewhat debilitating effect; after a lengthened minor, we rejoice once again to hear the major, which brings with it renewed vigour and freshness. The songs of the Northern nations, even the most joyous ones, are set in the minor keys. In one respect this seems to be an anomaly; and yet it can easily be explained. Partly it is the expression of sadness, of a people held in political serfdom; partly it emanates from the grave and melancholy character of the scenes amid which their lot is cast.

When the composer has chosen his key, he will be careful to handle it in such a manner that it does not attain too great a prominence, which would result in monotony, and cause fatigue and lack of interest in the listener; but he will manage to suffuse his work with the special characteristics of the key, which is thus made to glimmer or shine through the piece without asserting itself with undue strength. No better examples of such absolutely perfect and artistic treatment of the key could be found than that which we admire in Mozart's Symphony in G minor, in Beethoven's Symphony in C minor, and in the "Overture to the Hebrides" by Mendelssohn.

The task of marshalling different keys in a certain order, according to their characteristic qualities, is not only a matter of great difficulty but almost of impossibility, inasmuch as it cannot be denied that one composer detects in a certain key qualities which have remained entirely hidden from another. Mozart's Symphony in E flat is in no other way related to Beethoven's Eroica Symphony than that both are set in the key of E flat. And yet it cannot be denied that each key possesses distinctive characteristic qualities. If we maintain, for instance, that the "sharp" keys have a brighter, a more lively, and a fresher expression than those in flats, we lay down a rule which admits of many exceptions. All that we can safely do is to name the characteristic qualities of the keys as we deduce their characteristic expression from universally admired and accepted masterpieces: and thus we need not fear to misstate or to misapprehend the bearings of the subject.

C major expresses feeling in a pure, certain, and decisive manner. It is furthermore expressive of innocence, of a powerful resolve, of manly earnestness, and deep religious feeling. Examples: Mozart's aria "Dove sono" is redolent of pure feeling; his aria "Vedrai carino" is full of innocence; so is the "Chorus of the Maidens" in Weber's "Der Freischütz." Beethoven's Quintett (Op. 29) is full of manly earnestness, and Mendelssohn's air "Oh rest in the Lord" is expressive of the deepest religious feeling. Powerful resolve and manly earnestness shine forth in every note of the finale of Beethoven's Fifth Symphony, in Haydn's "The heavens are telling," and in Mendelssohn's "Lauda Sion."

C minor is expressive of softness, longing, and sadness; also of earnestness and a passionate intensity. At the same time C minor lends itself most effectively to the portraiture of the supernatural; as Weber has shown in the famous Incantation scene in "Der Freischütz." Examples: Schubert's "The Maiden's Lament" expresses a soft longing; the first movement of Beethoven's Symphony in C minor, and his Overture to "Coriolanus," convey through the key the impression of intensity and passion; the Funeral March of the Eroica Symphony impresses the listener by the solemnity and the dignified earnestness of the sombre key.

G major, that favourite key of youth, expresses sincerity of faith, quiet love, calm meditation, simple grace, pastoral life, and a certain humour and brightness. Examples: the well-known air "But the Lord," from Mendelssohn's "St. Paul," breathes true sincerity of faith; Don Ottavio's second air in "Don Giovanni" is expressive of quiet and devoted love; Mozart's Andante in six-eight time, from his Symphony in D major, is entirely characteristic of a calm and peaceful meditation; the same master's Finale from his celebrated String Quintett in G minor is a model of unadorned, genuine gracefulness; Rossini's "Ranz des Vaches," in his Overture to "Guillaume Tell," and Haydn's first chorus in the "Spring" of his "Seasons" give us splendid instances of faithful portraiture of pastoral life; the Finale of Beethoven's Fourth Concerto for the Piano affords an illustration of quaint humour; and as an unrivalled example of brightness we have Handel's chorus " See the conquering hero comes."

G *minor* expresses sometimes sadness, sometimes, on the other hand, quiet and sedate joy—a gentle grace with a slight touch of dreamy melancholy—and occasionally it rises to a romantic elevation. It effectively portrays the sentimental ; and when used for expressing passionate feelings the sweetness of its character will deprive the passion of all harshness and fierceness. Examples : Mozart's Symphony in G minor, Mendelssohn's sweet barcarole in the first book of his " Songs without Words," and Spohr's beautiful air " Onori militari," in his opera "Jessonda." This process of enumeration would result in a somewhat lengthy and confusing catalogue ; therefore I will merely state the qualities of the remaining keys, without supplementing them by examples.

D *major* expresses majesty, grandeur, and pomp, and adapts itself well to triumphal processions, festival marches, and pieces in which stateliness is the prevailing feature.

D *minor* expresses a subdued feeling of melancholy, grief, anxiety, and solemnity.

A *major*, full of confidence and hope, radiant with love, and redolent of simple genuine cheerfulness, excels all the other keys in portraying sincerity of feeling. Almost every composer of note has breathed his sincerest and sweetest thoughts in that favourite key.

A *minor* is expressive of tender, womanly feeling ; it is at the same time most effective for exhibiting the quiet melancholy sentiment of Northern nations, and, curiously enough, lends itself very readily to the description of *Oriental* character, as shown in Boleros and Mauresque serenades. But A minor also expresses sentiments of devotion mingled with pious resignation.

E *major*, the brightest and most powerful key, expresses joy, magnificence, splendour, and the highest brilliancy.

E *minor* represents grief, mournfulness, and restlessness of spirit.

B *major*, a key but seldom used, expresses in fortissimo boldness and pride ; in pianissimo purity and the most perfect clearness.

B *minor*, that very melancholy key, tells of a quiet expectation and patient hope. It has often been observed that nervous persons will sooner be affected by that key than by any other.

F sharp major sounds brilliant and exceedingly clear; as *G flat major* it expresses softness coupled with richness.

F sharp minor, that dark, mysterious, and spectral key, is at the same time full of passion.

C sharp major is scarcely ever used; as *D flat major* it is remarkable for its fulness of tone, and its sonorousness and euphony. It is the favourite key for Notturnos.

D flat minor, only used as *C sharp minor*, is undoubtedly the most intensely melancholy key.

A flat major is full of feeling, and replete with a dreamy expression.

A flat minor adapts itself well to funeral marches, and is full of a sad and almost heart-rending expression; in it we seem to hear the wailing of an oppressed and sorrowing heart.

E flat major is the key which boasts the greatest variety of expression. At once serious and solemn, it is the exponent of courage and determination, and gives to the piece a brilliant, firm, and dignified character. It may be designated as eminently a masculine key.

E flat minor is the darkest, most sombre key of all. It is but rarely used.

B flat major, the favourite key of our classical composers, has an open, frank, clear, and bright character, which also admits the expression of quiet contemplation.

B flat minor, a key full of gloomy and sombre feeling, like *E flat minor*, is but seldom used.

F major is at once full of peace and joy, but also expresses effectively a light, passing regret—a mournful, but not a deeply sorrowful feeling. It is, moreover, available for the expression of religious sentiment.

F minor, a harrowing key, is especially full of melancholy, at times rising into passion.

Some persons may have remarked the fact that our older masters wrote in a few keys only, and abstained from using keys with many sharps or flats. The reason for this abstinence was a mechanical one, and resulted from the imperfect state of the instruments in their time; the pieces also had to be adapted to the very imperfect technical execution of the orchestral performers. To thoroughly appreciate the true relation of the different keys with their various sentiments and feelings, no better example for study could be named than Beethoven's series of songs, "An die entfernte Geliebte." In this marvellous work Beethoven has bequeathed to us a true psychological study expressed in sounds. Nothing is here left to chance ; the sense of the words finds its truest expression in the well-selected character of the keys. Another study much to be recommended is the practice of transposing any favourite piece from its original key into another, to discover the difference of the effect. Another interesting study is that of different settings of the same words by various composers. We shall often find that the general character of a key may be changed by peculiarities and idiosyncrasies of the composer ; and· thus a key may appear to possess a cheerful character in the hands of one writer, whilst another composer infuses into it a melancholy expression ; all depends on the treatment, on the individual feeling of the composer, and on his acute understanding of all the different characteristic qualities of the key he employs. The modulations from one key into another depend very much upon the intensity of feeling in the composer. In this respect composers may be compared with painters, some of whom require brighter, some quieter colours, to portray their subject with perfect truth. In national songs, for example, we perceive but a limited use of modulations ; and even the most gifted composers, whose command over all the artistic means and resources is absolutely supreme, will, if they write in the mode of national songs, limit themselves to the most simple harmonies, and to a sparing use of modulations, so as truly and faithfully to preserve the national tone.

In so far as the words of the song are a decided form of expression, vocal music requires only a moderate use of modulations ; instrumental music depends much more on modulations, and, indeed, cannot dispense with their liberal use. But in this respect also we have to admire the wise moderation of our great composers, who were well aware that a too frequent use of modulations produces unsteadiness, indistinctness, and ultimate confusion.

The judicious and thoughtful composer will always know how to combine truth of expression with beauty of form, although too great an anxiety to render formal beauty prominent may sometimes weaken the immediate effect of the characteristic expression ; and for this reason we find that the best composers of instrumental music are not always the most successful writers of vocal music, and more particularly of songs.

We now have to examine the relations of the rhythmical to characteristic beauty. The rhythmical movement of music has to be considered as an expression of our inner life. Thus, as movement is always associated with physical life, certain phases of the life of the soul, of our inner consciousness, may be illustrated or described by music. It is natural and evident that such illustrations are represented by different kinds of rhythmical expression. The hearer feels sympathetically all that gives a characteristic importance and expression to the rhythm. We call the rhythm characteristic when it expresses in a correct and truthful manner the particular or especial feeling; and the rhythmical expression becomes *characteristically beautiful* when it is expressed in a free and intellectual manner.

In the commonest forms of musical expressions, in national dances, and in some of the national songs, we meet with an ordinary and rough kind of rhythmical expression. Even children, marching to or from school, or holding hands as they move round in a circle, instinctively keep time in their song. But here we must admire how this primitive and uncouth form of musical expression has been improved and refined by the genius of our composers. Although almost all our great writers have done something towards bringing this rhythmical portion of their art to perfection, we must accord the highest praise in this department to Mozart, Beethoven, and Weber, all of whom undoubtedly show in their works the greatest variety of rhythmical life.

The rhythmical movement exhibits itself in the emphasis, in the measure or bar, and in the time or movement. Generally speaking, the even measures, two-eight, two-four, and common time, appear more concentrated and precise than the uneven time of three-eight, and three-four, which express a vague and less intense feeling. The common or even time lends itself readily to the representation of passion and excitement; but on the other hand it is also expressive of quiet meditation or contemplation. Compare the most celebrated slow movements of Beethoven with each other, and it will be found that those written in two-four or common time express in a greater degree that peaceful tranquillity and undisturbed calmness, which may be considered the chief aim of the slow movement, than the slow movements written in three-eight or three-four time. We must except those adagios or largos in three-four time which move in so slow a manner that they almost entirely lose the characteristic of rhythmical movement. The two-eight and the two-four time differ from the common time by their greater vivacity and cheerfulness; two-four time in its original spondaic form possesses the least characteristic expression, and thus soon becomes monotonous; we generally find it in the national dances of those nations least endowed with natural musical feeling.

The two-four time expresses a certain cheerfulness; and if taken slowly it can express, in the happiest manner, a quiet, contemplative, even devotional feeling. Examples: the slow movement of Beethoven's A major Symphony, and of the same master's Adagio in his Sonata Appassionata; again, Beethoven, in the first movement of his celebrated Pastoral Symphony, found this two-four time best adapted to express truthfully and accurately "the awaking of cheerful sentiments on the arrival in the country;" and again we find that tender, sincere feelings, like those of Agatha in Weber's "Der Freischütz," or those of the page Cherubino in Mozart's "Le Nozze di Figaro," are most happily expressed in this time.

The common time expresses the quiet life of the soul, a solid earnestness, an inward peace—but also strength, energy, and courage. Passion, expressed in common time, will be a passion confined within reasonable bounds. Almost all the grand, majestic music that our great composers wrote, the majority of hymns, chorales, and solemn choruses, have been set in common time; and there is no doubt that the elevated and superb, the powerful and the deepest feeling, expresses itself in this time with an even balance, and with a decided beat or rhythm. Examples: Handel's "Hallelujah Chorus," the "March of the Priests" in Mozart's "Il Flauto Magico," and the Finale of Beethoven's C minor Symphony.

The three-eight time expresses joy, a bright and sincere pleasure, which less affects our feeling, than it carries us insensibly along in an unpretending and agreeable manner. It also lends itself admirably to scherzos. But when the three-eight time is used for describing passion, it is remarkably expressive of suddenness and impulse; and when employed in dance movements, these will soon degenerate into the expression of a frantic excitement, and of a kind of bacchanalian frenzy, and result at last in a wild noise and tumult. The best and most beautiful characteristic of this kind of time is that of innocence, and the charm of simplicity. Examples: Zerlina's Air, "Vedrai carino;" Beethoven's Andante, Second Symphony, and Andante in F.

The three-four time expresses in a mitigated form all that the three-eight time expresses passionately. The three-four time is also expressive of longing, of supplication, of sincere hope, and of love. It possesses singular tenderness and a remarkable fund of romantic expression. It lends itself also very effectively to the description of sincere devotional feelings, and has therefore been often most happily used in sacred music. When applied to dance-music it impresses us with a certain dignity combined with an easy grace; the regular German valses, the polonaises, the boleros, and other dances are set in this time.

The six-eight time is the natural interpreter of a spontaneous joviality and pleasure; but it also unites gracefulness with dignity, and may sometimes be used as expressive of a mournful senti-ment; yet the sorrow it indicates is rather that of young persons, who do not yet feel so deeply and intensely as their elders. Example: Pamina's Air in G minor in Mozart's "Il Flauto Magico."

The six-eight time is the favourite time for national songs, and hunting-songs, for barcaroles, and similar compositions. When it occurs as six-four time it obtains a much greater dignity, a certain broad and even pompous and majestic flow. Examples: Weber's overture, "Ruler of the Spirits," and Mendelssohn's Forty-second Psalm.

The nine-eight time is mostly used for depicting quiet grief and calm melancholy. Beethoven has given us a beautiful specimen of these characteristic qualities in the short movement descriptive of the death of Clärchen, in Goethe's tragedy of "Egmont."

The twelve-eight time may be described as covering the widest space, and is particularly adapted for expressing copiousness of thought and a certain wealth of invention in the composer; at the same time it lends itself especially to the description of sincerity and grandeur. Beethoven, in his Pastoral Symphony,

uses the twelve-eight time to express the good-natured contentment and the genial feeling of the people in the scene near the
brook. Again, the twelve-eight time appears with great effect
in the Lacrymosa of Mozart's " Requiem ; " and there can be no
doubt that the first movement of Beethoven's Sonata Appassionata
truthfully expresses an earnest and sincere feeling.

Specimens of mixed times are found in Mendelssohn's Overture
to " Ruy Blas," where the most impassioned allegro is suddenly
interrupted, as if at the word of command, by the magnificent
lento. Spohr, in his much admired Symphony " The Conse-
cration of Sounds," Mozart, in the first finale of " Don Giovanni,"
and Beethoven, in the latter part of the scherzo of his Eroica
Symphony, have each and all furnished excellent examples of the
effective use of this natural, yet stirring, means of expression.

The respective movements of time may be classified under five
heads : first, the very slow movements ; second, the moderately
slow movements; third, the moderately quick movements ; fourth,
the quick movements; and fifth, the very quick movements. Under
the first head are comprised *largo*, " broad ; " *largo assai* and the
adagio, " very broad "—the word *adagio* comes from the verb
adagiare, which means " to take one's ease ;" *lento* means
" slow, idle, dragging ;" and *grave*, " grave and heavy."   The
moderately slow movements are *larghetto*, " a little broad ;"
andante (from *andare*, " to go ")—it should be not fast, but certainly
not dragging ; *andantino* is the diminutive of *andante*, and its
movement is consequently less quick than that of the andante,
although *andantino* is generally, but erroneously, taken as
a quicker time than the andante ; *sostenuto* means " held
back, sustained," showing a lingering on the movement ; and
commodo means " easily, pleasantly."   The moderately quick
movements are *allegretto*, " a little lively ;" *moderato*, " with
a moderate movement ;" *allegramento*, " in the manner of an
allegro ;" *allegro moderato*, " moderately quick ;" *allegro ma non
troppo*, " quick and lively, but not in too great a degree." The
quick movements are *allegro*, which means " cheerful and
lively ;" *animato*, " animated ;" *allegro con brio*, " with freshness ; " *allegro con moto*, " with a lively movement ;" *allegro con
fuoco*, " quick, with fire ;" *allegro agitato*, " agitated ;" and *allegro
appassionato*, " with a passionate movement." The quickest
movements are *allegro assai* or *allegrissimo*, " very lively and

very quick ;" *allegro vivace*, " with vivacity ;" *vivace* and *viva-cissimo*, " exceedingly quick " and " with extreme vivacity ;" and *presto, presto assai*, and *prestissimo*, "quick" " exceedingly quick " and " as quickly as possible."

Although the composer designates by the above names the time in which he wishes his composition to be performed, the performer, on the other hand, has to consult his own taste and feeling in modifying the prescribed movement. C. M. von Weber says truly that " there is not a single slow movement in which passages do not occur which demand a greater anima-tion ; and, *vice versâ*, that there is not a single quick movement which would not at times demand a certain slackening of the time." The *tempo rubato*, however, which actually means "stolen time," is inadmissible ; in short, any dragging or quickening of the time which does not originate in the absolute feeling or in the character of the piece, and which appears entirely as the result of the peculiar or individual taste of the performer, is devoid of artistic feeling, and destroys truth and correctness. One of the happiest musical effects consists in the simultaneous application of a slow and a quick movement, a slow and a quick time together. Example : the duet of Agatha and Annie in Weber's " Der Freischütz," in which Agatha, with her loving and sorrowful heart, sings in a slow movement, whilst the bright and somewhat mischievous Annie warbles her brilliant scales in quite a lively strain.

As in speaking, the proper accentuation and emphasising of words will assist the hearer to understand the meaning of the sentence, so in music the *accent* helps the hearer to seize the real meaning of a phrase, to understand what may be called the plastic form of the composition. As in speech, so in music accentuation is indispensable. In songs, the accent is suggested by the words ; in instrumental music, however, it originates in the feeling ; the accent gives to music the characteristic design, invests it with importance, and becomes ultimately an individual language of the soul.

The syncopated passages (those in which the accent is trans-posed) are a development of the ordinary accent ; and, if sparingly used, may produce the happiest effect. In fact, it is by a judicious and tasteful combination of tones, or again by an appropriate division of them, and by a judicious prominence given to a certain

note, that the piece receives the proper life, the effective light
and shade. The accent is in music what a ray of light is in
painting. It gives life to the whole. But besides giving
clearness, the accent may impart a certain liveliness, charm,
interest, and originality. The principal fascination of modern
French music, for instance, is to be found in the sometimes highly
original accentuation of the different phrases. Examples are seen
in Auber's operas.

The pause is not merely a necessity, but may be made the
vehicle of the greatest effect. The listener's attention at times
demands a certain rest ; and such a rest seems requisite to allow
the auditory impression to die away, so as to leave the ear free
to appreciate the next effect. A continued movement may be
followed with undivided attention for a certain time; but when
the limit of the hearer's power of concentration is reached, there
must be a pause, or fatigue and even indifference will follow. It is
related that Mozart was asked what in his opinion produced the
greatest effect in music. "No music," was the laconic reply.
He meant the cessation of music. But a pause does not only act
beneficially; it likewise depicts the greatest excitement, heightens
the expectation of the hearer, and is particularly effective in
sacred music. The sudden cessation of glorious sound produces
an impression of awe, and gives the hearer a moment to realise
the sensation the music has produced on his mind. Again, in a
piece which expresses the wildest passion, a sudden pause may
indicate terror, shuddering, and fear. It is like the sudden
suspension of the beating of the heart ; when the pulsation stops
and life seems for the moment to be arrested. Haydn, on the
other hand, succeeded in extracting a comical effect from the
pause. In some of his symphonies and quartetts the unexpected
pauses produce an intentionally whimsical expression.

In the *melody*, characteristic beauty shows itself most promi-
nently ; and this beauty does not consist only in the greater
or smaller distance between the different notes, but also in the
combination of the tones into figures, which fill the rhythmical
space commonly called the bar. It is the expression, the intellectual life of the principal theme, which gives the characteristic
colour to the piece ; while the logical and clear relation of the
minor or tributary melodious phrases to the principal subject
strengthens and intensifies the character of the whole work.

But precision and correctness of accent are indispensable in the principal theme, as without these we should not be able to understand the logical sequences that result from the principal subject.

It is evident that a well-chosen harmonisation must greatly help to give due prominence to the accent ; *characteristic beauty* has its basis in *formal beauty.* The composer uses the form, replete as it is with beauty and variety, free life and harmony; and with this he unites truth of *expression*—which union will result in a more striking, vivid effect. But it may also happen that the characteristic element preponderates in such a degree that the formal element appears only as a secondary or minor feature. We have instances in which this preponderance of the one element over the other appears entirely to disturb the necessary balance ; and when this is the case an unsatisfactory patchwork will be the result.

But again, we may point out examples which show that the characteristic element may possess such irresistible charm and power, that the occasional absence of the formal element is wholly unnoticed. No one will deny that Weber's overtures to "Oberon," "Euryanthe," "Der Freischütz," &c., carry us away with an irresistible might, and excite us to real enthusiasm ; yet, were we to compare their formal construction with that of the overtures of Mozart or Beethoven, we should find them somewhat inferior. It was certainly in the characteristic expression, full of life and animation, replete with truth and correctness, that Weber displayed and cultivated his chief strength ; and his Huntsmen's Choruses, the Incantation scene in " Der Freischütz," the romantic feeling of Adolar in the opera " Euryanthe," and the delicious, fairylike tone of the " Oberon " music, are marvels of characteristic beauty.

A classification of the different means for characteristic expression is exceedingly difficult. The impressions that dwell in our soul and heart, that linger in our memory, that excite our intellect, are inexpressibly varied ; and only the artist, who clearly understands his own innermost feelings, and is able to realise them, will find the suitable means to express these feelings in an outward form.

If we divided the domain of our feelings as it were into provinces, we should find a region of hidden or suppressed activity, grief, and passion ; again, a free and elevated life,

c

bursting forth in joy and cheerfulness. Our soul may be alternately swayed by feelings of seriousness and mirth, solemnity and cheerfulness, dignity and carelessness, reality and dreams ; and for each of these phases of feeling music possesses an adequate expression. But were we to attempt to lay down a theoretical rule, and, for instance, to declare that devotion, solemnity, grief, must be expressed in long and heavy notes, or in a slow succession of chords—and cheerfulness and brightness in quick notes, with shakes and runs—we should give but a poor and very incomplete description of the musical means, because the same means of expression may produce very different effects. Thus we find, for instance, that a tremulous movement may at one time express agitation and anxiety, and at another may very effectively portray the grand and sublime. It is always a difficult problem to unite the general with the specific ; only when the *individual* feeling of the composer is thoroughly suffused and penetrated by the *general* feeling, and only when it recognises the absolute laws of nature, will a true and thoroughly effective work of art be the result. The composer has to see that the form he has chosen for his representation contains and reproduces with correctness and truth all that the feelings of the soul and the psychological laws require.

Truth of expression is therefore an absolute necessity. A composer who introduces brilliant and florid passages into an air which is to describe pious and sincere devotion will simply produce an absurd effect. Yet our greatest masters have sinned in this respect ; and the only excuse they can plead for such offences against natural rules is the necessity of complying with the tyrannical dictates of a fleeting taste and fashion.

Chromatic passages afford very effective means for characteristic expression. They can be used to illustrate the uproar of the elements, the feeling of sorrowful anxiety, and the storm of angry passions. If written in a slower time, they easily degenerate into sickly sentimentality, into a morbid expression, and soon become monotonous. Chromatic passages may be used most effectively to describe something mysterious, something that is merely whispered, and is supposed to remain a secret. Too liberal an application of chromatic passages deprives the piece of its characteristic colour. In painting, the chromatic science is actually that of mixing the colours.

Enharmonic changes are often happily applied, and highly suggestive of a sudden change or an unexpected impulse. Again, if harmonies are varied on one and the same tone, they express the greatest solemnity, and sometimes gloom and dismay. Examples: Schubert's song, " Death and the Maiden," and the warning of the Commander in " Don Giovanni."

Not every figure possesses in itself a characteristic expression ; only when the figure is properly used, and when it is combined with harmony and melody, does it become of great, almost of supreme importance. It will then intensify and heighten the character of the melody, and can never fail to increase its beauty. It will float round the melody as the graceful folds of a veil encircle a charming face; it furnishes a relief that takes away all appearance of bareness or poverty from the theme.

Sincerity and purity of feeling will always produce the greatest effect in music. We often find that the simplest and most entirely unadorned national song awakens our sympathies, whilst a carefully elaborated work may leave us cold and indifferent. Our enjoyment certainly reaches the highest point, if to the sympathy which a work arouses in our mind is added an intellectual interest; we seem to be initiated into a kind of mystery, which we are by degrees able to solve, and whose intricacies we can unravel.

The different voices offer to the composer a rich mine of characteristic expression, by their varied application. Soprano, contralto, tenor, and bass, have each their own specific character. The soprano voice is expressive of a lofty and graceful feeling; the contralto voice portrays the sentiment of resignation, of a subdued earnestness, of consolation ; the tenor voice expresses passion, ardent love, and manly courage ; the bass voice, again, is redolent of dignity, solemn earnestness, severity, and warlike ardour.

The different instruments possess each a separate characteristic expression; and the happiest effects sometimes result from a union of the human voice with an obbligato instrument. Example : Zerlina's Air, " Batti, batti," in which she tries to conciliate the jealous Masetto ; the cordial, honest-toned violoncello seconds her supplications most effectively. It helps to soothe Masetto's anger and assists in pouring oil on the troubled waters of his wrath. Again, the wonderful soprano Air in B minor in Sebastian Bach's St. Matthew Passion, is admirably supplemented by the solo violin, which, with sustained and expressive tones, brings out in its greatest intensity the pervading feeling of grief and genuine sadness.

The instruments afford to the composer inexhaustible and ever-varying means of characteristic expression. We might truly say that every instrument has a soul of its own, which has its bright and dark phases; and the proper and thorough study of the nature of the instruments might not inaptly be compared to the psychological studies of the philosopher; the surprising effects some composers have drawn from the resources of the instruments warrant us in supposing that a rigorous study, a complete abandonment to the earnest part of the art, is necessary for the recognition of all the manifold beauties which lie hidden in the instrument. And how interesting, how suggestive is the fact that one and the same instrument shows quite different qualities under the appreciative genius of different composers! The flute, which accompanies Pamina on his passage through water and fire in Mozart's " Il Flauto Magico," is a very different instrument from Mendelssohn's fanciful reed in the incomparable scherzo of his " Midsummer Night's Dream " music. The oboe of Haydn is quite different from that of Auber. Spohr's clarionet has little affinity with that of Beethoven. The instruments are indeed to the musician what colours are to the painter.

CONCLUDING REMARKS ON CHARACTERISTIC BEAUTY.

We thus find that music speaks its own language in the characteristic element; a language not indeed so distinct and precise as human speech, but one that, on the other hand, soars to heights which human language can hardly attain. The sounds cannot indeed describe distinctly and literally the entire thought that filled the brain of the composer during the progress of his work; but they undoubtedly express his feelings, and excite in us, the listeners, an intellectual activity, an earnest sympathy. Every feeling and every emotion that reigns within the vast regions of our inner spirit-world proves its existence through the characteristic, which again uses for its representation *expression*, with all the various means we have named. Character is the chief and principal condition for the existence and appearance of a tone-picture ; it is the most important element of a musical work of art, the one which most surely arouses our sympathy and interest.

All that is characteristically correct and true is in itself beautiful. It pleases, without requiring to be examined with our reasoning faculties ; it acts immediately on our feeling ; on hearing it our interest is thoroughly aroused, and the chords of our soul vibrate irresistibly. We have seen that there is a great difference between *general* and *musical* ideas. The former result from logical reasoning, and may be evolved from mathematical rules ; the latter, on the other hand, are the offspring of the real and sincere feeling, and thus possess a greater charm, a higher beauty, a deeper intrinsic power. All who feel in a lively, quick, and ready manner will instinctively understand characteristic expression. It will speak to them in an intelligible language ; in short, it will be felt and appreciated, though they may not understand the process. The mental qualities which are necessary for the proper study and recognition of the different elements of the beautiful in music are a quiet power of contemplation, and an innate sense of order and symmetry for the appreciation of the *formal* beauty ; a lively fancy, quick perception, and spontaneous feeling for the conception of the *characteristic* beauty ; and elevation of mind, purity of soul, and innate enthusiasm for all that is good and noble, for the proper recognition of *ideal* beauty.

III.

IDEAL BEAUTY.

If we accept the maxim often enunciated—that beauty does not exist where every one of its elements is not present in a higher or lower degree, and that the special beauty of any particular work lies, therefore, not in the presence, but in the predominance of one of the elements of beauty—it follows that we must consider ideal beauty as a particular and special expression of the beautiful, and also as one of the principles which must penetrate every beautiful and perfect work of art. When the sculptor presents in his work absolute formal beauty, when the painter gives in his picture a characteristic and faithful reproduction of the important inner life, they have both given specimens of real beauty considered from the respective points of view—the formal and the characteristic; their productions will be regarded as something important, and will be praised and valued accordingly. And yet, in the work of neither does the highest beauty appear, in its absolute essence, and in its fulness. Real life has here clothed itself in a beautiful form, and expresses pleasantly the importance of an intellectual activity; but material nature cannot be divested of its reality, nor can the limits of the actual be exceeded.

But now we will suppose a third and a higher quality united with the formal and characteristic beauty; and let this third quality penetrate the before-mentioned representation of nature with an ideal inspiration—let there appear in the artist's work the predominating principle of *ideal beauty*—and then the beauty that will result will be of the highest kind, and absolutely complete and perfect. That animation which impresses upon the work the stamp of the infinite comes immediately from the ideal world; from ideas, which are present in the domain of the intellect, which soar above reality. The infinite appears in the beautiful, and the idea receives a perceptible and intelligible form, when the soul of the composer reveals itself with the greatest clearness; since the representation of the illimitable— the perfectly and purely intellectual—awakens presentiments of the soul, which cause it to soar beyond the limits of time and space, and transport it into an invisible and inaudible world ; since feelings are thus expressed and suggested, through which the distant regions of the infinite announce themselves and appear to us like a halo—a glory surrounding the heights and depths of nature.

This element of the infinite can never be entirely absent in a beautiful work, even though that work be but a simple national song, a pastoral scene, a sweet tune ; for if this element is absent, the work cannot in the higher sense be beautiful, though on the other hand the ideal is not always recognised. It may be present in so small a degree that it fails to be distinctly perceived,— and being hidden by the other features, those of the formal and the characteristic beauty, it is overlooked. We are therefore, in matters of beauty, entitled to recognise a *higher* or *lower* degree, a *lofty* or a *moderate* standard. While the character-

istically beautiful expresses something peculiar in its nature, and
reproduces fact, the ideal, on the other hand, raises us into the
sphere of the universal, and endeavours to seize in pictures the
lofty meaning of the ideas, which appertain to the domain of
symbolic representation. And this symbolic significance is
peculiar to the ideal phase of the beautiful.

This idea of the three kinds of beauty, the formal, the
characteristic, and the ideal, may be readily explained by an
analogy drawn from a sister art, that of painting. Three
pictures may be presented to our notice: the first represents,
we will say, a boy—a lovely form, showing, in its outlines
and in its free grace, proportion and completeness of design
penetrated by *life*. This is a picture of *formal* beauty, and
pleases through the literal charm of its outward loveliness.
In the second picture, let there be represented once more the
same boy, but not alone ; now he is wrestling with another boy.
They are in full activity; and in every line, and in the bodily
action of each, is expressed youthful vigour, and a certain
exuberance of effort ; this second is a *characteristic* picture, and
excites the interest of the looker-on by its vigorous life. In the
third picture, let the boys appear once more ; but they are here
shown as beings of a higher order, not belonging to common
humanity ; they are represented as genii or angelic spirits, as
denizens of a higher world; in fact, they are idealised. Something
purely intellectual, not borrowed from nature, is here represented.
One of the figures, we will say, holds aloft a palm branch, the other
strives to grasp it ; but this action expresses a hidden meaning,
and the spectator tries to understand the mystery of the symbolic
incident he finds represented. Thus also feelings, pronounced
in music, may express themselves in a lofty manner that seems
to elevate the hearer above the real and actual. Beethoven's
symphonies may be cited as works possessing *ideal* beauty in
the highest degree.

But not only Beethoven possesses this elevated feeling ;
Mozart, Bach, Handel, Haydn, may also be credited with it. If
we analyse, for example, Sarastro's air in "Il Flauto Magico"
we must at once admit that it belongs to the domain of ideal
beauty. We do not recognise in Sarastro the priest of the
temple of Isis : he appears before us as the representative of the
high and holy in humanity. In Haydn's chorus, "The heavens

are telling," we hear a hymn of praise sung by creation in honour of the Eternal. Just as deeply are we moved by Handel's "Messiah;" by the opening chorus of Bach's St. Matthew Passion; by Elijah's air, "It is enough." The intense devotion of a broken and contrite heart; the utterances of a soul which prays for wings, to be enabled to soar from this nether world to happier, brighter regions; and the three sweet voices which bring consolation to the aching heart of the Prophet, seem in reality the voices of angels. Thus also, in many of Schubert's and Schumann's songs, we find traces of undeniable ideal beauty; and, indeed, were we to examine some of the greater works more closely and diligently, instead of giving ourselves up wholly to the charm of enjoyment—were we to analyse our feeling and exert our intellect—we should discover many a beauty which lies hidden, and does not reveal itself to the superficial hearer. He only who penetrates into the heights and depths of the ideal can understand its true meaning.

No supposition could be more erroneous than that which would limit ideal beauty to serious, grand, or sacred compositions. Ideal beauty can be contained in a scherzo, a minuet, and even in still shorter and lighter forms. Equally erroneous is the notion that ideal beauty necessarily shows itself in everything that is original.

If such false maxims were followed out to their ultimate consequences, we might go so far as to call everything beautiful that is strange and odd, curious and unexpected—everything that sets the customary rules at defiance, or that exhibits unusual harshness; and thus we should consider eccentricity as naturally belonging to the domain of ideal beauty. Daily experience proves that an unpoetical farrago and an unmusical confusion of sounds arrest the attention of the uneducated masses; and we have too many examples of the fact that admiration of the extravagant and the unusual can become a fashion. We often find that people seek the ideal in the combination of materials, even of heterogeneous materials, which are in themselves dull and lifeless; and such people think that a great victory has been achieved by collecting and throwing together these worthless elements. But on closer examination we shall recognise the shallowness and worthlessness of such productions, as the intellectual essence never appears in them, for the simple reason that it does not exist. If, on the one side, the law of ideal beauty demands a defined and a pure form and perfect clearness, so, on the other hand, no variety of devices, were they ever so various—no use of the most far-fetched effects—will supply the place of the pure intellectuality and vastness, whose expression is found in the ideal.

Every art employs the simplest means for attaining ideal beauty, which is its culminating point; and each has generally obtained a favourable result, in proportion as it has been able to combine a certain number of important elements into harmonious unity. Shakespeare's Imogen appears in her simplicity, gracefulness, and pure softness as a really ideal picture, whilst many tragical characters, overflowing with rhetorical and bombastic phrases, fail, notwithstanding their varied flourishes and their seeming superabundance of power, to impress themselves on our souls.*

In ideal beauty each work of art reaches its climax, its highest point of perfection; and it is by means of ideal beauty that the composer is able to raise us above the sublunary sphere of actual life into the higher regions of the sublime. The effect which this ideal beauty produces on an educated mind will rise in proportion to the fulness with which the ideal has been felt and understood. It is only through the inward feeling of the soul that we can follow the ideal; for the colder power of the intellect is incapable of receiving and assimilating the thought whose very essence and characteristic consists in the fact that it cannot be subjected to the analysis of measure and of rule. A Don Giovanni in real life would, at best, awaken in us a kind of amused curiosity not unmingled with contempt; neither his character nor his adventures would arouse in our hearts anything akin to a feeling of sympathy; but in Mozart's opera he

---

* Beethoven could not have chosen anything more unpretentious and simple than the subject for the minuet in his Eighth Symphony; and yet he succeeded in filling the little work with ideal beauty. In its transparent clearness it developes a most important unity. The trio of the minuet may be called a model of ideal beauty, combined with the most unpretending simplicity; the effect is in the first instance produced by two horns and one clarionet, round which the violoncello, as a faithful companion, weaves a figure in triplets; then the violins come in and give the melody in C major, afterwards transposing it into the key of A flat, and ultimately bringing it back in the most natural harmonious order, but withal in a most artistic and intellectual manner, into the principal key of F, where the horns take up the subject again.

approaches us, and becomes not an example to be imitated or
avoided, but simply the exponent of some very charming music.
He is thus entirely an ideal creation. A second work of the same
master, " Il Flauto Magico," contains many characteristic and
also many ideal beauties, which, if the beauty as appreciated by
the ear is separated from the impression made upon the eye,
moves the hearer so spontaneously that all connection with the
outward and real will be forgotten. Often the characteristic
serves as a foundation to the ideal ; but the former recedes to
such a degree as to leave the individual expression of the
composer as the great and prominent feature. This is the basis
of all the rules of ideality, which latter does not merely consist in
an ennobling and beautifying of the natural, but soars to the
higher regions of the imaginative, and looks from earth to
heaven. Right well has Shakespeare said :—

> The poet's eye, in a fine frenzy rolling,
> Doth glance from heaven to earth, from earth to heaven,
> And, as imagination bodies forth
> The forms of things unknown, the poet's pen
> Turns them to shapes, and gives to airy nothing
> A local habitation and a name.

In Beethoven's Pastoral Symphony the characteristic beauty is
throughout a prominent feature; but no one would dare to assert
that because this is the case this masterwork is destitute of the
higher or ideal beauty. We have already stated that a work of
art receives its highest stamp from the ideal ; but ideality is in
fact present in such a marked degree in everything that is
beautiful that nothing can, strictly speaking, be called really
beautiful where ideality does not leaven the mass. It must be
present, and, though it may show itself only in a minor degree,
it must nevertheless animate the whole in every really beautiful
work of art. To an artistic mind, to an appreciative spirit, even
this impalpable essence will be discernible, although it will not
obtrude itself or even obtain general recognition. Indeed, in
speaking of the appreciation of ideal beauty we may use the
words of the poet Cowper, and say, as he says of conversation,
that though this appreciation

> In its better part
> May be esteemed a gift, and not an art;
> Yet much depends, as in the tiller's toil,
> On culture, and the sowing of the soil.

The composer whose works may be taken pre-eminently as a type of ideal beauty in music is Beethoven. This master possessed in an eminent degree the powerful intellect, the depth of feeling, and the warmth of enthusiasm which combine to make up the perfect composer. His special domain, the region in which he worked and created, was the ideal. This fact shows itself in the animation of his melodies, which glow with a higher power that, as it were, transforms his sounds into loftier utterances; it reveals itself through the mighty efforts with which he dives into the very depths of the soul, and brings to light its hidden treasures—efforts in which we find a reflection of a supernatural world, and from which there shines forth the reflex of a great and noble life, with all its joys and all its sorrows. With him the intellectual, the grand and genial, as exhibited in the modulations and combinations of sound, oversteps the regular form, and is not the result of a passing mood of feeling, or of chance moments of inspiration; it is, in fact, the exhibition of tone-pictures, all possessing the richest fulness of power, and revelling in an inexhaustible wealth of variety, in which they strike on our enraptured ear. With respect to that wonderful genius, Schiller's lines in his poem, " The Ideal and the Actual Life," are exceedingly appropriate :—

> For never, save to Toil untiring, spoke
>   The unwilling Truth from her mysterious well ;
> The statue only to the chisel's stroke
>   Wakes from its marble cell.
>
> But onward to the sphere of beauty ! Go
> Onward, O Child of Art ! and, lo,
>   Out of the matter which thy pains control,
> The statue springs ! Not as with labour wrung
> From the hard block, but as from Nothing sprung,
>   Airy and light, the offspring of the soul !
>
> The pangs, the cares, the weary toils it cost,
>   Leave not a trace when once the work is done ;
> The artist's human frailty merged, and lost,
>   In Art's great victory won !

The faults which have been imputed to Beethoven, and which appear perhaps here and there in his works, are faults arising neither from ignorance nor from negligence; but they are the idiosyncrasies and peculiarities which may never be wholly dissociated from the human intelligence, when it soars away on the track of ideal enthusiasm. "The giants must live alone." They are above ordinary mortals and ordinary rules. There may be condemned before the tribunal of criticism, for incorrectness or for a forbidden licence, many a passage which revealed itself to the composer's spirit during its highest flight, and appeared to him combined in a unity far above the conditions of daily rule or common perception. It has been said in some quarters that Beethoven's works, here and there, exhibit too great an elaboration, resulting in a want of unity : but the critics who thus judged these works did not consider that so full an energy, and so deep a conception of the importance of the world of ideal feeling, required for its expression a larger space, and a steadily increasing wealth of material. In the last years of his life, this craving for melody increased in Beethoven to the highest degree, even to an extreme ; there arose in him an absolute desire that everything, even minor parts, and secondary, and supplementary instruments, should *sing*. But, in spite of the carpings of dissatisfied critics, there can be no doubt that the sonatas, quartetts, and symphonies of Beethoven contain a sequence and a series of harmonies, which seem to include in themselves a whole world of music ; they unfold ideal designs which no abstract process of intelligence can correctly explain or satisfactorily interpret.

As the ideal beautiful is founded on the accurate and truthful expression of the purely intellectual and the absolute, and thus the content of the representation appears subjected to, and influenced by, the varying views natural to the human intellect, it naturally results that the difference between the fashion of the old and the modern time, and the position which mankind maintained in the different conditions of life, must have a great and lasting influence. The art of the ancient ages, and particularly that of old Greece, showed the ideal beauty as a rounded and complete symbol of the infinite and divine ; and if this was realised in its greatest extent, in the objective plastic art, and in epic and dramatic poetry, we may reasonably assume that music, which at that time was confined more to the rhythmical, possessed an expression, or rather a suggestion, of ideal beauty.

But when music became the vehicle for the elucidation of the inner life of the soul, so rich in presentiments of a higher destiny

—when it had to portray feelings, too deep to be expressed in words—when the sentiments of devotion and love were awakened by a higher revelation of religion—then our delightful art became able to give an ideal tendency to its productions.

By degrees the art advanced, and took full advantage of this element, obtaining it chiefly through the discovered wealth of harmony, which, at first uncouth and consequently simple and poor, as we find it appearing in the most ancient sacred hymns, in due time proceeded to build up the noble structure on a characteristic foundation, and succeeded, by the combination of the most various means, in expressing all the phases of feeling which embrace the idea of the Sacred, Divine, and Eternal—all the feelings which we recognise in the sublime works of Bach, Handel, Mozart, Haydn, and Beethoven.

It will be well now to revert for a time to the point from which we started. A work of art deserves the epithet *perfect*, and its beauty may be considered as the *highest*, when the three elements of the formal, characteristic, and ideal appear in complete purity; and when there is manifested a free and intellectual nature in the proportions of the form, in the portraiture of the peculiar life, and in the revelation of the lofty and infinite ; and when it thus entirely satisfies the requirements of the contemplative mind.

If one of these elements appears in greater prominence, or even gives to the work its tone and expression, we are thus justified in calling the whole or part of it, according to the particular sphere in which it moves, either formally, characteristically, or ideally beautiful.

It is not the aim of music to imitate the appearances of reality, as is continually done in painting, sculpture, and architecture, or to transport reality into the intellectual spheres ; music finds its vocation in this, that it firmly seizes the life of the human soul with its sorrows and joys ; and, subjecting these feelings to the idea of the beautiful, represents by sounds the expressions of individual truth, and, as it were, the presentiment of an infinite life.

To contemplate these different beauties—to examine, to find out which of the different elements preponderates, or in which part of a work they appear simultaneously—all this affords to the judicious mind refined pleasure of the highest order. Not only do we penetrate into the mysteries of the art in general, but we become acquainted with the individual qualities of the composers, we take a natural interest in the development of their intellectual faculties, we try to find out the circumstances which influenced the composition of such or such a work. Indeed, the veil is lifted from our eyes, we see clearly and distinctly; and the power of insight we thus acquire, the improved acuteness of our critical faculties, far from rendering us more realistic, enhances our love for the art, increases our sincere admiration for those, its votaries, who fulfilled their mission with such devotion, with such pure and lofty enthusiasm.

Uneducated intellects will never reach the pure heights of perfection. He who aims at the greatest, the highest, must summon all his strength. The real master shows himself ready to submit to natural restrictions ; it is only through the honest observance of the laws and the rules of art that we can obtain real and true freedom. The history of art tells us how, according to the time and the national influences brought to bear, one or other of the three elements of beauty predominated, and served as the basis of the productions.

In music and painting the characteristically beautiful is the first achievement which appears. In painting, it manifests itself in pictures of religious subjects ; in music, it appears in the form of songs of the people. Both these arts pursued the same course and reached the goal—music in the so-called tone-painting, the pictorial art in the allegorical treatment of the subject. Italian music always leaned towards formal beauty ; German music, taken from a general point of view, inclined towards the characteristic ; but in all great composers, whether Italian or German, existed the consciousness that the highest perfection could only be obtained by that ideal life which gives to works of art elevation, purity, and lasting fame.

In one respect only the beauty of art surpasses that of nature herself; and this applies not to musical art especially, but to art in general. In saying that art surpasses nature, we do not assert this because a statue, for example, has a longer existence than the human being it represents ; but for another, and a higher reason. A great philosopher, Schelling, has remarked : " Every product of nature has only one single moment of perfect beauty, namely, the moment of its highest development, the culminating point of its entire life, just as the sun has only one moment in which it reaches its highest point in the heavens. Only in the one moment of highest development is a natural product what it ought to be according to its design; before and after this moment we recognise in it a growth and a decline." And this culminating moment of nature can be seized by the artist. It ought to be sought out, so to say, from the life, and ought to be fixed. This is the true idealisation; this is the real, the only faithful portraying of nature; for the power of invention is a faculty which resides by nature in the human soul, and acts voluntarily; and this advantage artistic beauty has, that it can perpetuate and retain in permanence the fleeting charm that nature possesses. Foremost in all other respects, art has yet to take nature as the highest, truest model, and must submit to her rules.

It is the aim of true art to reproduce the original beauty of the products of nature, and more particularly to idealise and perpetuate human beauty. Art has to exhibit to humanity the ideal picture of what perfect human beauty can be.

It is evident that religion and art are closely connected; and we find from history that art, which originated in religion, meets it again as it runs its course, and assists religion faithfully in its great mission to ennoble and purify the moral and intellectual faculties of mankind. Art, when separated from religion, becomes vapid, and loses its highest application. Religious services, deprived of art, would lose a valuable means of lifting the souls of worshippers to higher aspirations and emotions. The service of religion is the highest aspiration of art. Art, again, may be the "decent and seemly" garment of religion. Art, like religion, conceives and creates from the infinite; and therefore we find that the truest and greatest artists were sincerely religious, perhaps not in a conventional, but certainly in the substantial point of view; for history testifies that an artist without sincere religion has never raised himself above the worldly spirit of his time.

The effect which a real work of art produces depends on the feeling of affection or sympathy. If such sympathy is evoked, the result will be that the hearer will experience the same feeling by which the composer was inspired during the creation of his work; and this feeling in the hearer is called admiration. These feelings of sympathy and admiration are an indestructible part of human intelligence; they afford the purest and sincerest joy to the heart,—they raise us above all the barriers of time and space. Music has become so popular, it has obtained such undisputed supremacy as a means of amusement and enjoyment, and sometimes of education and refinement, that we often forget to consider whence comes its surprising effect, its irresistible strength. Thousands of people rush to concerts and to operas, are delighted with the sweet sounds, the rich harmonies, the enchanting melodies which salute their ears; yet not one in each thousand will take the trouble to analyse the source of his enjoyment; and many, even if they endeavoured to do so, would be unable to account for it. In musical art nothing is left to mere chance. The composer has not only to learn all the hundreds of rules which regulate the prosaic part of his work, but he has to study nature; he must dive into the psychological mysteries of the human heart, must identify himself with the feeling which his subject demands; in short, the composer has to pass many an anxious hour, before he can lay his pen down with the consciousness that he has faithfully served his art, that he has made good use of the talent which a Divine Power intrusted to his care.

Therefore it should be the duty and the privilege of the student to do everything in his power to make himself worthy of the noble and rich legacy bequeathed by the great masters,—by trying with zeal and heartiness, with energy and perseverance, to recognise all that is beautiful and admirable in the great works of our magnificent composers, and by seeking to deserve the praise which, in Goethe's "Apotheosis of the Artist" the Muse grants to the young painter :—

> Within his eye the heartiest wish doth shine,
> To catch the impress of thy soul divine.
> And thus, with might, each noble man
>   For centuries doth work upon his kind.
> For what a good man's power can do and plan,
>   Ye cannot in a life's short limit bind.
> Therefore, e'en after death hath closed his eyes,
>   He lives, in good for which he's striven ;
> The lofty deed, the noble word, ne'er dies—
>   The gift's immortal, though by mortal given.

NOVELLO, EWER AND CO., Printers, 69 and 70, Dean Street, Soho, W.

www.ingramcontent.com/pod-product-compliance
Lightning Source LLC
Chambersburg PA
CBHW031823090426
42739CB00008B/1387